My Book of Numbers

Mi Libro de los Números

SOUTHWESTERN

My Books
© 2013 Southwestern Advantage
Nashville, Tennessee
ISBN 978-0-87197-583-6
Reprinted in 2019

Dustin Hillis
Chief Executive Officer,
Southwestern Family of Companies

Dan Moore
President, Southwestern Advantage

Curriculum Director
Janet D. Sweet

Art Director
Travis Rader

The publisher would also like to thank
the original creators of this book:

Editorial Team
Mary Cummings • Judy Jackson
Barbara J. Reed

Art and Design Team
Steve Newman • Starletta Polster
Matt Carrington

Printed in China

SWAdvantageOnline.com

Contents / Índice

Skwids.com

The Ones That **Start** Ahead...Stay Ahead!

- Skwids video lessons, games, and quizzes provide the essential skills needed for success in school.

- Skwids tracks progress and tells you what your child knows and what they should focus on next.

- Skwids teaches important life lessons, too, for emotionally well-rounded kids.

- Skwids makes learning fun so kids stay engaged in the process at school and at home.

Download the **Skwids App!** Kids can watch favorite episodes wherever they want, whenever they want!

Note to parents
Nota para los padres

Congratulations on choosing the *My Book* series for nurturing your child's vocabulary development! Learning to read is an exciting time for you and your child, and vocabulary development is an essential first step in early reading success.

Southwestern Advantage understands that young children are naturally drawn to images, words, and ideas that are all about their world. The *My Book of Numbers* features bright-colored art and vibrant illustrations to encourage your child to explore the familiar, high-interest words and concepts used in everyday life.

Your child will also enjoy the lovable Skwids characters from Southwestern Advantage's early learning website, www.skwids.com, as they introduce each category of vocabulary words. Learn more about Kangaroo, Monkey, Giraffe, and the other Skwids characters as they weave the concepts from the *My Books* series—and other Advantage book series—into fun early-learning videos, games, songs, and more!

We are committed to helping our youngest learners develop early reading success and a zest for learning. So turn the page and enjoy an important step in learning to read!

Janet D. Sweet
Curriculum Director

Felicidades en escoger la serie de libros *My Book* para estimular el desarrollo del vocabulario de su hijo. El aprender a leer es una etapa excitante para usted y su niño. El desarrollo del vocabulario es el primer paso esencial para el éxito temprano en la lectura.

El Southwestern Advantage entiende que los niños son atraídos de una forma natural a imagines, ideas y palabras acerca de su mundo. El libro *My Book of Numbers* ofrece arte con colores brillantes e ilustraciones para estimular a su niño a explorar palabras familiares de alto interés y conceptos del diario vivir.

Su niño va a disfrutar de los personajes adorables Skwids del website de Southwestern Advantage, www.skwids.com cuando le introducen el vocabulario en cada categoría. Aprenda sobre los personajes Kangaroo, Monkey, Giraffe y otros caracteres en el Skwids cuando les presenten los diferentes conceptos en la serie de libros *My Books* y en otra serie de libros Advantage—ten videos divertidos de aprendizaje temprano, juegos, canciones y mas!

Estamos comprometidos a ayudar a nuestros niños pequeños para que tengan éxito temprano en la lectura y un deseo de aprender. Así que pase la pagina y empiece a disfrutar en este paso importante en el aprendizaje a leer.

Janet D. Sweet
Curriculum Director

Introducing numbers
Presentamos los números

Numbers can tell us "how many." How many objects do you see in this picture?

Los números pueden indicarnos cantidades. ¿Cuántos objetos ves en este dibujo?

four balloons
cuatro globos

one unicycle
un monociclo

three
plates
tres
platos

five clubs
cinco
bolos

two pies
dos
tartas

Numbers 1–10
Los números del 1 al 10

We can write numbers using symbols.
Each symbol stands for a certain amount.

Podemos escribir los números usando
símbolos. Cada símbolo representa una
determinada cantidad.

1 **one**
uno

2 **two**
dos

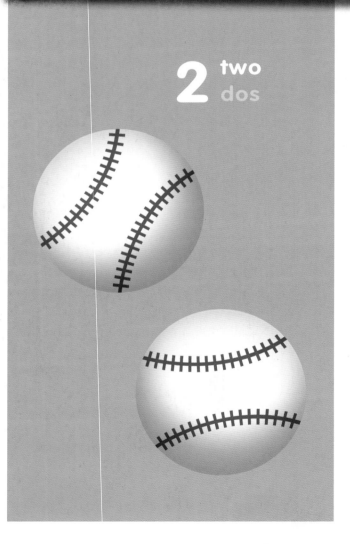

3 **three**
tres

4
four
cuatro

one
uno

two
dos

three
tres

four
cuatro

5 five
cinco

6 six
seis

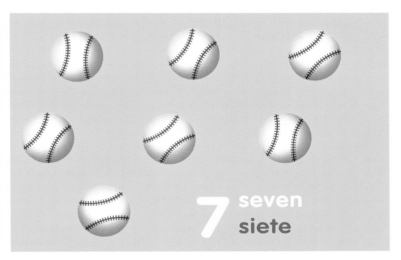

7 seven
siete

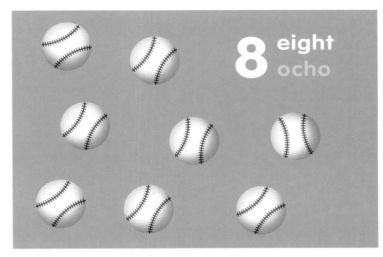

8 eight
ocho

9 nine
nueve

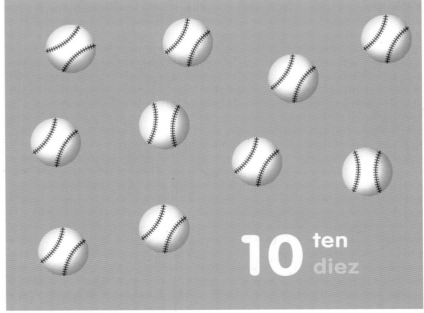

10 ten
diez

| **five** | **six** | **seven** | **eight** | **nine** | **ten** |
| cinco | seis | siete | ocho | nueve | diez |

Count the fruit.
Cuenta las frutas.

1 melon
melón

2 pineapples
piñas

3 apples
manzanas

4 oranges
naranjas

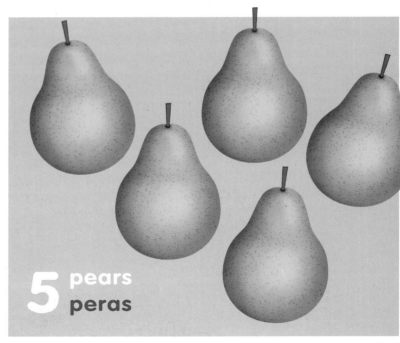

5 pears
peras

melon	pineapples	apples	oranges	pears
melón	piñas	manzanas	naranjas	peras

6 bananas
bananas

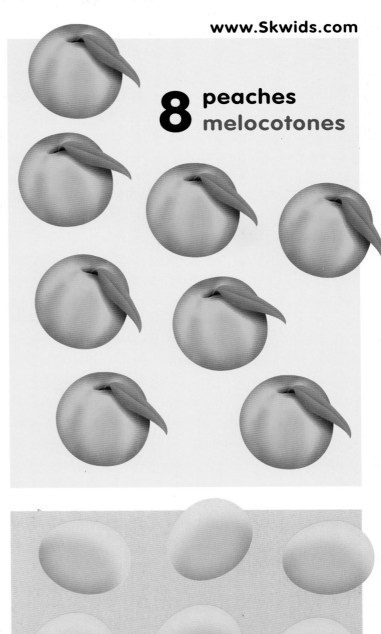

8 peaches
melocotones

7 cherries
cerezas

9 blueberries
arándanos

10 grapes
uvas

bananas bananas	**cherries** cerezas	**peaches** melocotones

blueberries arándanos	**grapes** uvas

Count the animal babies.
Cuenta los animales bebés.

1 foal
potrillo

2 puppies
cachorros

3 lizards
lagartijas

4 kittens
gatitos

5 bunnies
conejitos

foal	puppies	lizards	kittens	bunnies
potrillo	cachorros	lagartijas	gatitos	conejitos

6 chicks
pollitos

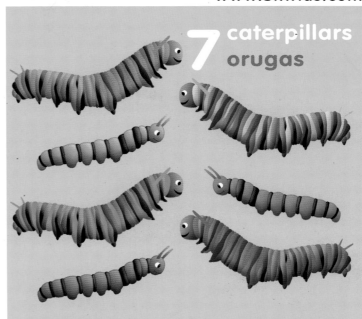

7 caterpillars
orugas

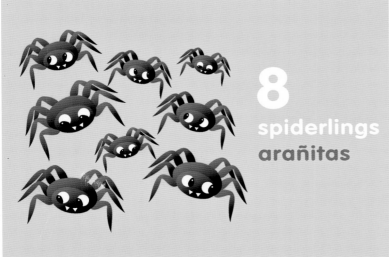

8 spiderlings
arañitas

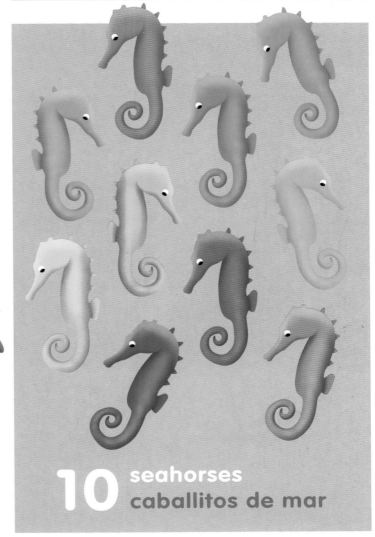

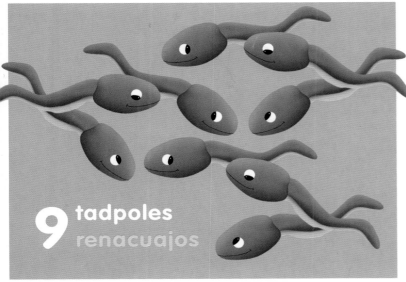

9 tadpoles
renacuajos

10 seahorses
caballitos de mar

chicks	caterpillars	spiderlings	tadpoles	seahorses
pollitos	orugas	arañitas	renacuajos	caballitos de mar

Count the legs.
Cuenta las patas.

lion
el león

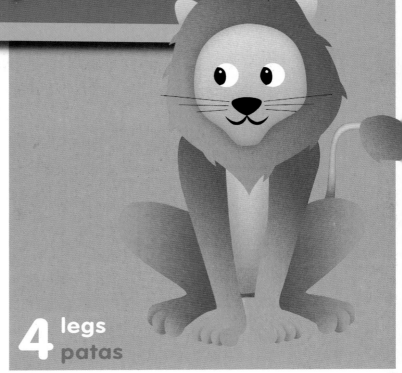

beetle
el escarabajo

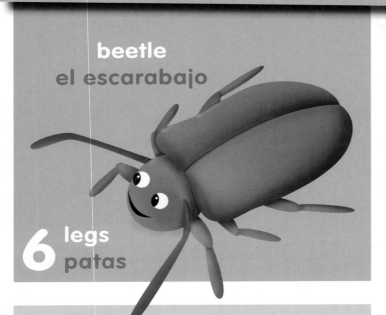

6 legs
patas

4 legs
patas

bird
el pájaro

2 legs
patas

10 legs
patas

crab
el cangrejo

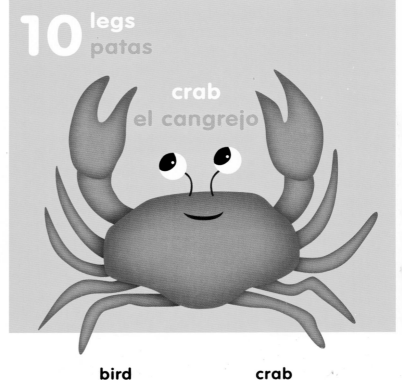

14

beetle	lion	bird	crab
el escarabajo	el león	el pájaro	el cangrejo

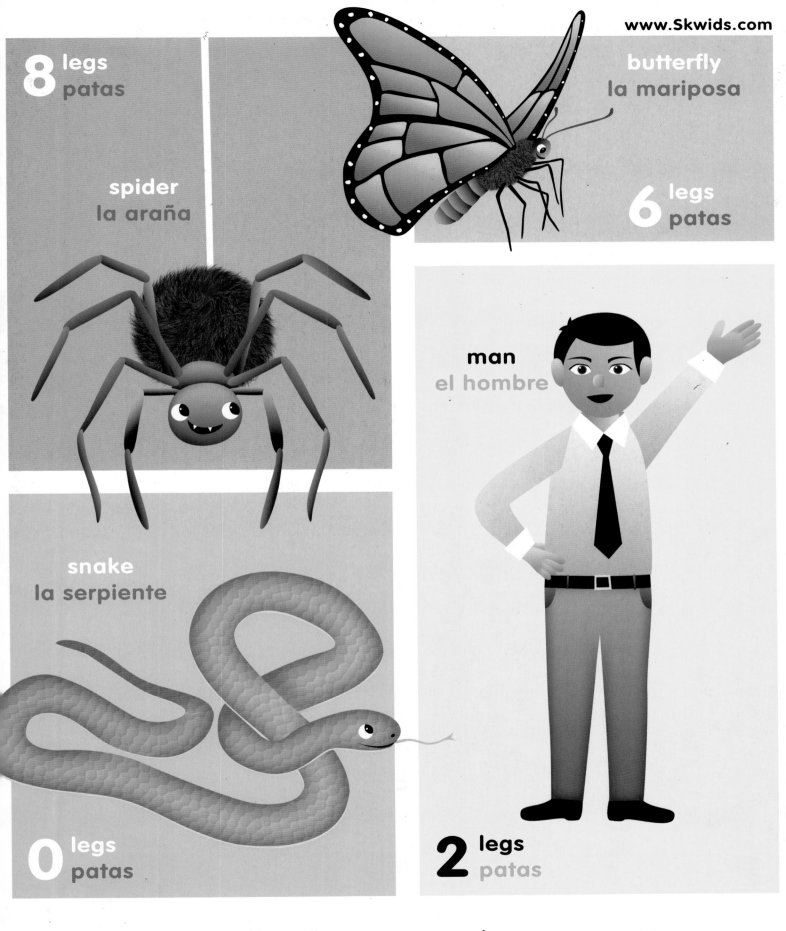

8 legs
patas

spider
la araña

butterfly
la mariposa

6 legs
patas

man
el hombre

snake
la serpiente

0 legs
patas

2 legs
patas

| **spider** | **butterfly** | **snake** | **man** |
| la araña | la mariposa | la serpiente | el hombre |

Adding by 1
Sumando de a 1
Count the objects in each panel.
Cuenta los objetos de cada panel.

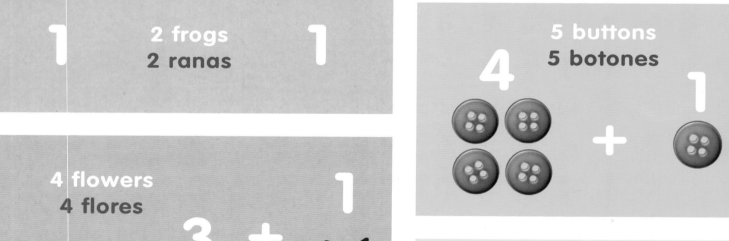

2

3 t-shirts
3 camisetas

1

1 + **1**

2 frogs
2 ranas

5 buttons
5 botones

4 + **1**

4 flowers
4 flores

3 + **1**

6 marbles
6 canicas

5 + **1**

| **frogs** | **t-shirts** | **flowers** | **buttons** | **marbles** |
| ranas | camisetas | flores | botones | canicas |

6 + 1

7 toy cars
7 autos de juguete

7

| 15 | 10 | 5 | 1 |
| 50 | 5 | 15 |

+

1

25

8 stamps
8 estampillas

8 + 1

9 ice cream cones
9 conos de helado

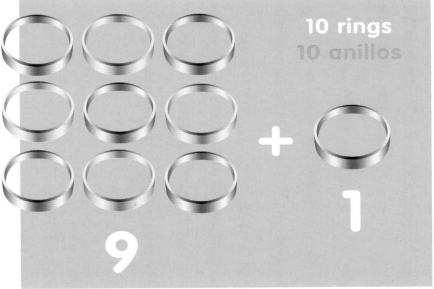

10 rings
10 anillos

9 + 1

| toy cars | stamps | ice cream cones | rings |
| autos de juguete | estampillas | conos de helado | anillos |

Numbers in a desert
Los números en un desierto

Deserts are full of numbers. Count the different animals and plants in the big picture.

En los desiertos hay muchos números. Cuenta los distintos animales y plantas en el dibujo grande.

three birds
tres
pájaros

one mountain
lion
un puma

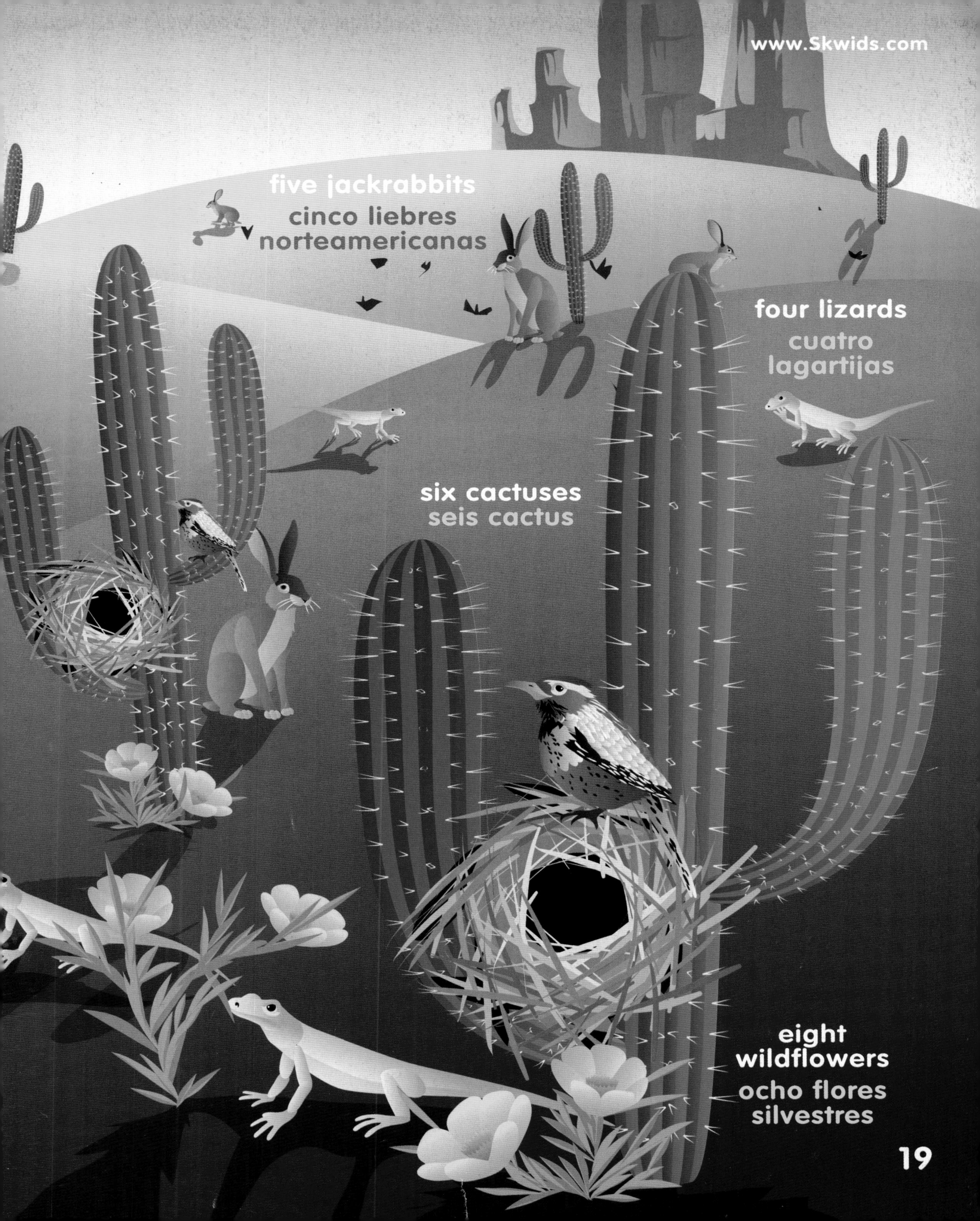

five jackrabbits
cinco liebres
norteamericanas

four lizards
cuatro
lagartijas

six cactuses
seis cactus

eight
wildflowers
ocho flores
silvestres

Numbers 11–20
Los números del 11 al 20

Can you count to 20?
¿Puedes contar hasta 20?

11 eleven
once

12 twelve
doce

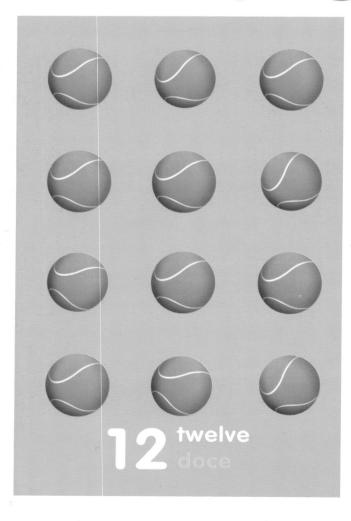

13 thirteen
trece

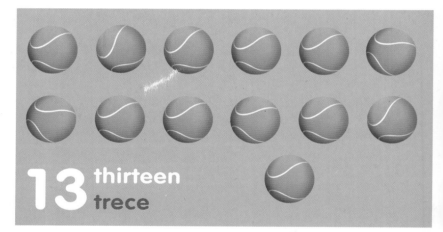

14 fourteen
catorce

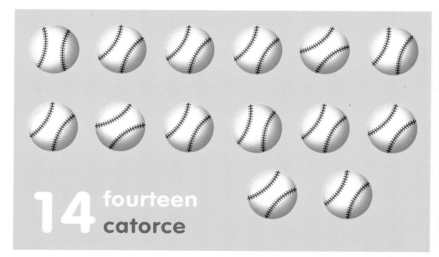

eleven	twelve	thirteen	fourteen
once	doce	trece	catorce

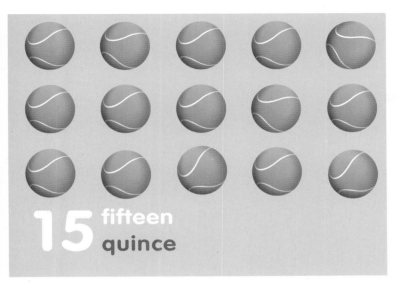

15 fifteen
quince

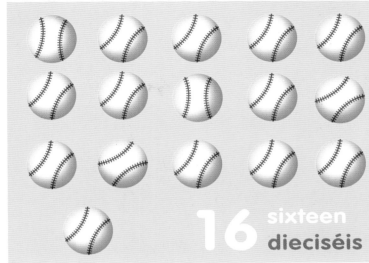

16 sixteen
dieciséis

17 seventeen
diecisiete

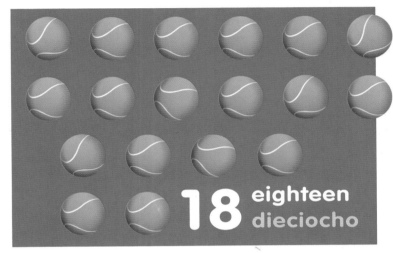

18 eighteen
dieciocho

19 nineteen
diecinueve

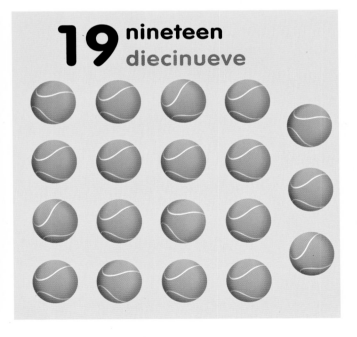

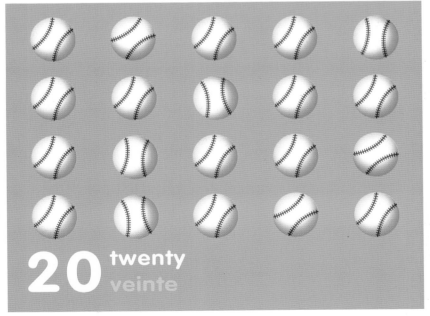

20 twenty
veinte

fifteen	sixteen	seventeen	eighteen	nineteen	twenty
quince	dieciséis	diecisiete	dieciocho	diecinueve	veinte

Count the school supplies.
Cuenta los útiles escolares.

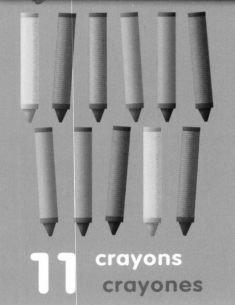

11 crayons
crayones

12 pieces of paper
papeles

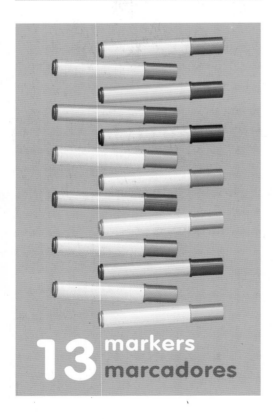

13 markers
marcadores

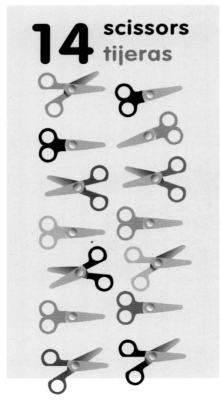

14 scissors
tijeras

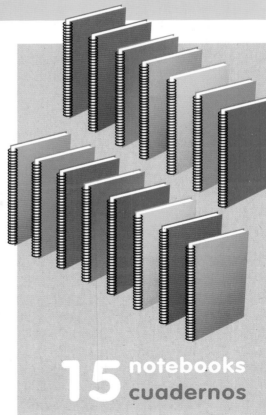

15 notebooks
cuadernos

crayons	pieces of paper	markers	scissors	notebooks
crayones	papeles	marcadores	tijeras	cuadernos

16 calculators
calculadoras

17 pieces of chalk
tizas

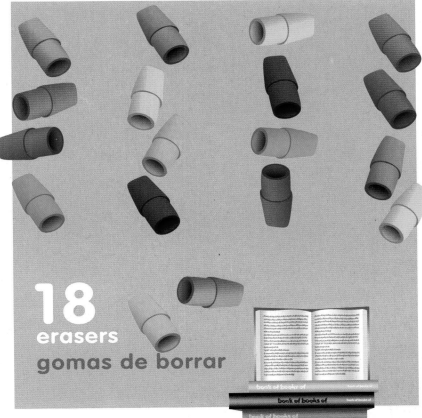

18 erasers
gomas de borrar

19 rulers
reglas

20 books
libros

calculators
calculadoras

pieces of chalk
tizas

erasers
gomas de borrar

rulers
reglas

books
libros

23

Count the musical instruments.
Cuenta los instrumentos musicales.

11 **drums**
tambores

12 **violins**
violines

13 **flutes**
flautas

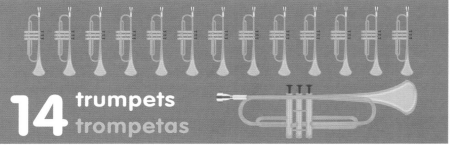

14 **trumpets**
trompetas

15 **guitars**
guitarras

drums	violins	flutes	trumpets	guitars
tambores	violines	flautas	trompetas	guitarras

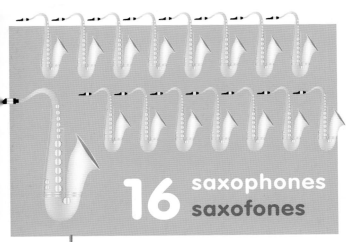

16 saxophones
saxofones

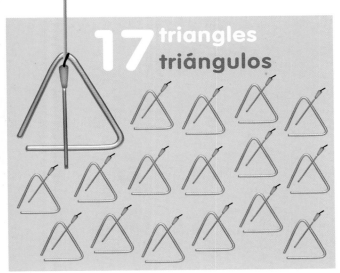

17 triangles
triángulos

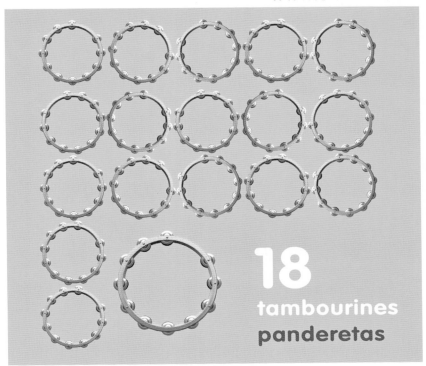

18 tambourines
panderetas

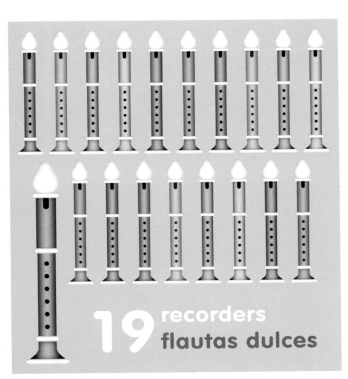

19 recorders
flautas dulces

20 keyboards
teclados

saxophones	triangles	tambourines	recorders	keyboards
saxofones	triángulos	panderetas	flautas dulces	teclados

Counting by 2's
Contando de a 2

Can you count by 2 up to 20?

¿Puedes contar de 2 en 2 hasta 20?

4 scooters monopatines

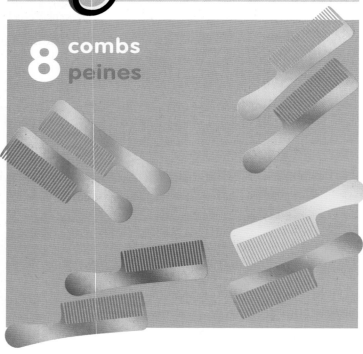

2 tables mesas

6 soccer balls pelotas de fútbol

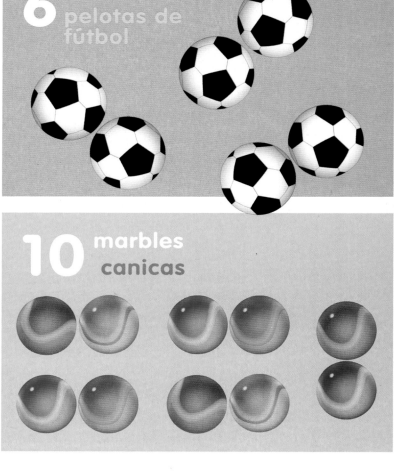

8 combs peines

10 marbles canicas

tables	scooters	soccer balls	combs	marbles
mesas	monopatines	pelotas de fútbol	peines	canicas

12
candles
velas

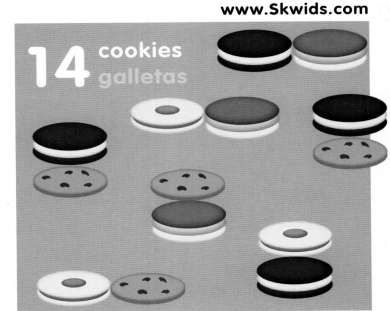

14 cookies
galletas

16 glasses
lentes

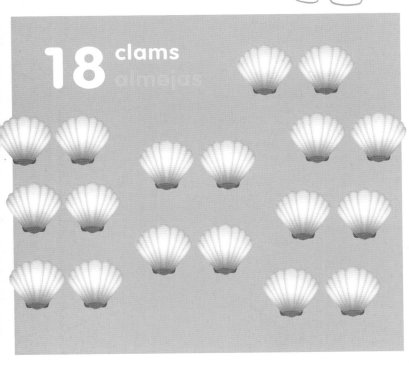

18 clams
almejas

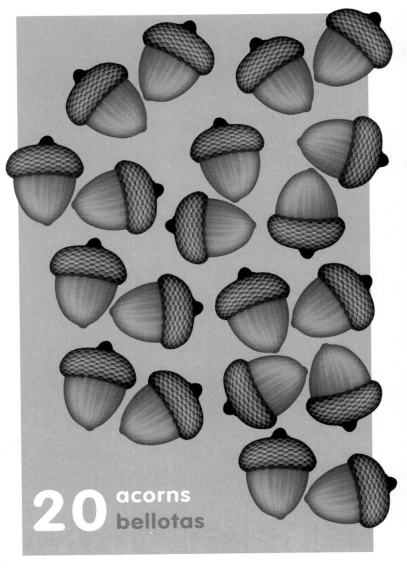

20 acorns
bellotas

candles	cookies	glasses	clams	acorns
velas	galletas	lentes	almejas	bellotas

27

How many pairs?
¿Cuántos pares hay?

A pair is a set of two things that go together. Count the pairs in each panel.

Un par es un grupo de dos cosas que van juntas. Cuenta los pares en cada panel.

1 pair of eyes
par de ojos

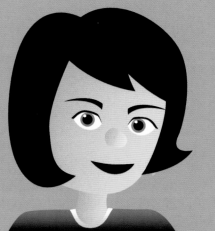

2 pairs of wings
pares de alas

5 pairs of chopsticks
pares de palillos chinos

6 pairs of skates
pares de patines

| **eyes** | **wings** | **chopsticks** | **skates** |
| ojos | alas | palillos chinos | patines |

8 pairs of socks
pares de calcetines

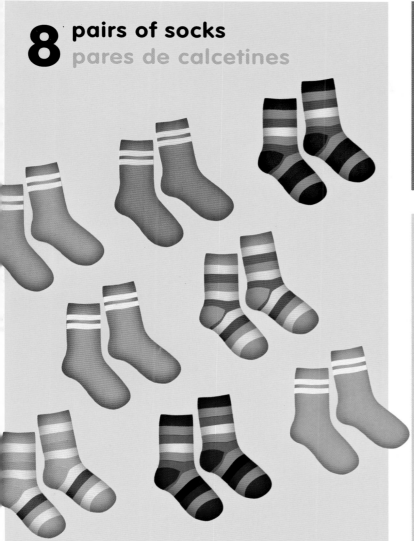

10 pairs of earrings
pares de aros

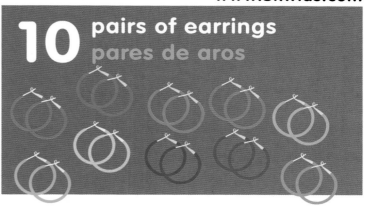

11 pairs of gloves
pares de guantes

13 pairs of pants
pares de pantalones

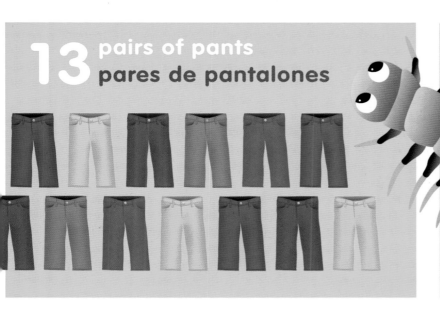

15 pairs of legs
pares de patas

socks	earrings	gloves	pants	legs
calcetines	aros	guantes	pantalones	patas

Which is more?
¿Cuál es más?

Look at the two sets of objects in each panel. Then decide which set has more objects.

Mira los dos grupos de objetos en cada panel. Luego, decide qué grupo tiene más objetos.

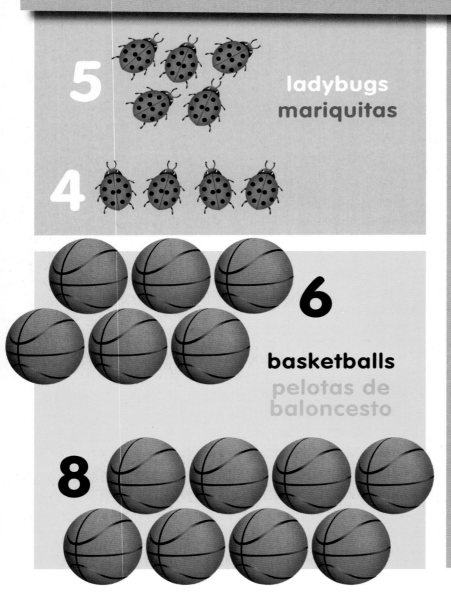

5 ladybugs mariquitas

4

6 basketballs pelotas de baloncesto

8

2 cupcakes pastelitos

3

ladybugs
mariquitas

cupcakes
pastelitos

basketballs
pelotas de baloncesto

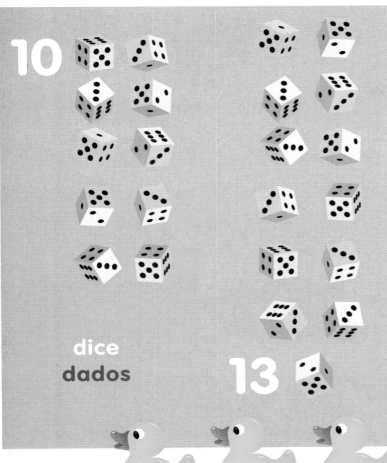

10

dice
dados

13

8

dolls
muñecas

9

7

rubber ducks
patitos de goma

11

dice	dolls	rubber ducks
dados	muñecas	patitos de goma

Which is biggest?
¿Cuál es más grande?

Look at the objects in each panel. Can you find the biggest object? Count the objects that are the same size.

Mira los objetos en cada panel. ¿Puedes encontrar el objeto más grande? Cuenta los objetos que tienen el mismo tamaño.

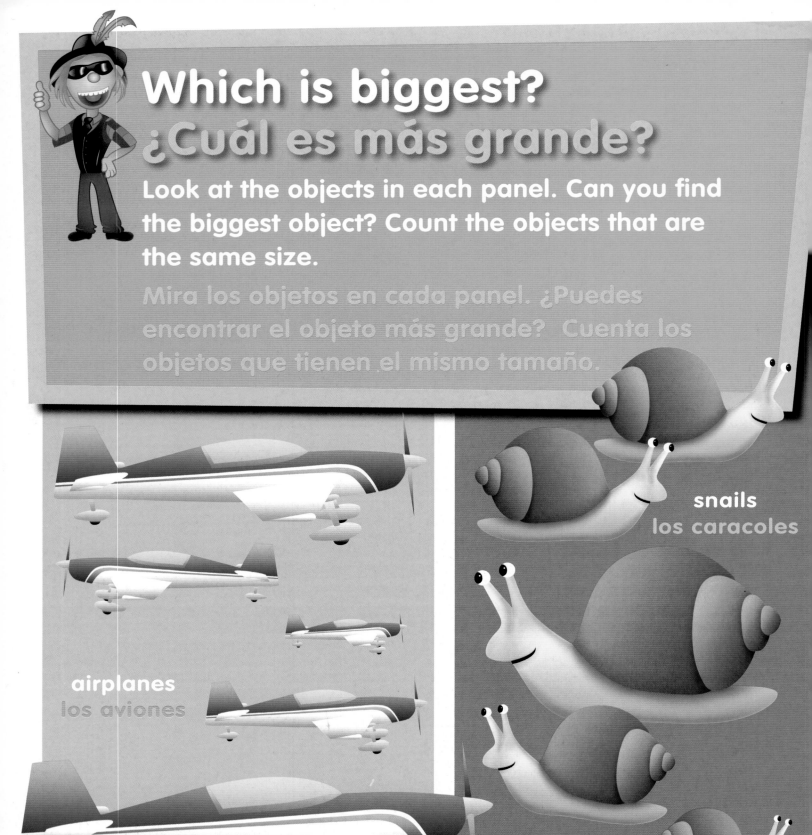

snails
los caracoles

airplanes
los aviones

airplanes
los aviones

snails
los caracoles

beach balls
las pelotas de playa

fish
los peces

trees
los árboles

beach balls
las pelotas de playa

fish
los peces

trees
los árboles

33

Spot the difference!
¡Encuentra la diferencia!

The panels on these pages show objects that are not quite the same.

Los paneles de estas páginas muestran objetos que no son exactamente iguales.

snakes
serpientes

Which snake has the most stripes?
¿Qué serpiente tiene más rayas?

Which scarf has the most spots?
¿Qué bufanda tiene más manchas?

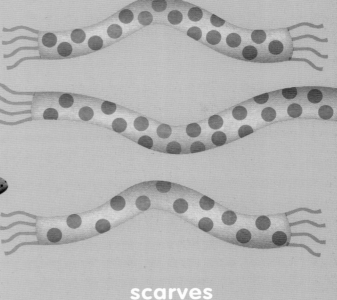

scarves
bufandas

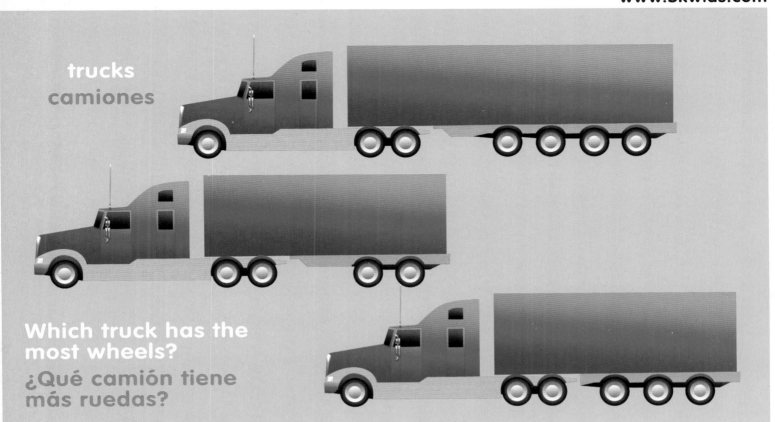

trucks
camiones

Which truck has the
most wheels?

¿Qué camión tiene
más ruedas?

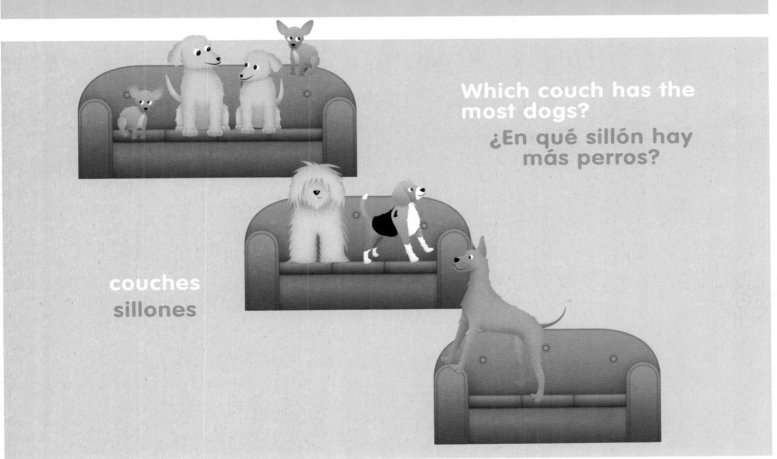

Which couch has the
most dogs?

¿En qué sillón hay
más perros?

couches
sillones

trucks
camiones

couches
sillones

35

Telling time
Decir la hora

We use numbers to tell time. What times do these clocks show?

Usamos los números para decir la hora.
¿Qué hora muestran estos relojes?

twelve o'clock
las doce en punto

one o'clock
la una en punto

two o'clock
las dos en punto

three o'clock
las tres en punto

four o'clock
las cuatro en punto

twelve o'clock	one o'clock	two o'clock	three o'clock	four o'clock
las doce en punto	la una en punto	las dos en punto	las tres en punto	las cuatro en punto

five o'clock
las cinco en punto

six o'clock
las seis en punto

seven o'clock
las siete en punto

eight o'clock
las ocho en punto

nine o'clock
las nueve en punto

ten o'clock
las diez en punto

eleven o'clock
las once en punto

five o'clock	**six o'clock**	**seven o'clock**	**eight o'clock**	**nine o'clock**	**ten o'clock**	**eleven o'clock**
las cinco en punto	las seis en punto	las siete en punto	las ocho en punto	las nueve en punto	las diez en punto	las once en punto

37

Counting money
Contar el dinero

We use money to buy food, clothing, and other goods. We also use money to pay for services, like going to the doctor.

Usamos el dinero para comprar comida, ropa y otros productos. También usamos el dinero para pagar por servicios, como la visita al médico.

1 cent
centavo

5 cents
centavos

10 cents
centavos

25 cents
centavos

1 dollar
dólar

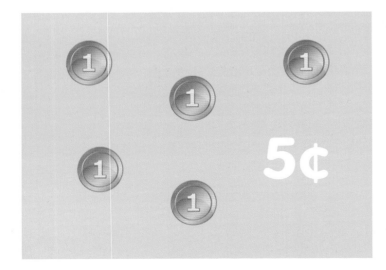

5¢

10¢

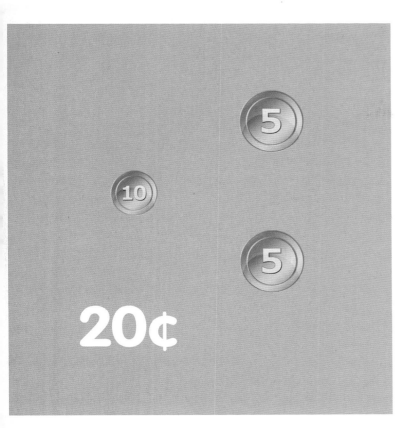

20¢

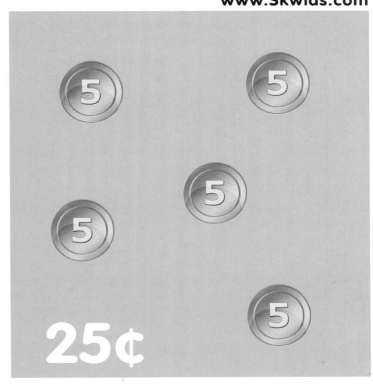

25¢

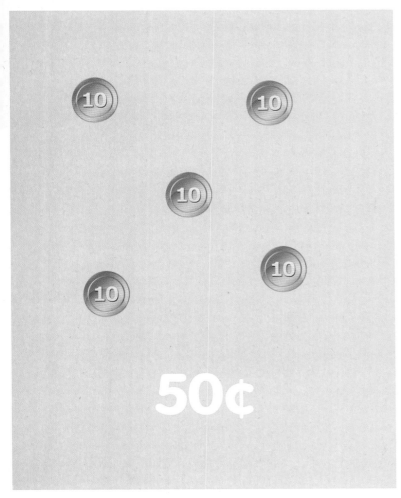

50¢

$1

In what order?
¿En qué orden?

The picture on these pages shows people who have just finished a race. Who finished the race first?

El dibujo de esta página muestra a las personas que acaban de terminar una carrera. ¿Quién terminó la carrera de primero?

first
primero

second
segundo

third
tercero

fourth
cuarto

fifth
quinto

sixth
sexto

seventh
séptimo

eighth
octavo

ninth
noveno

tenth
décimo

Numbers in a neighborhood
Los números en un vecindario

How many numbers can you find in the big picture?

¿Cuántos números puedes encontrar en el dibujo grande?

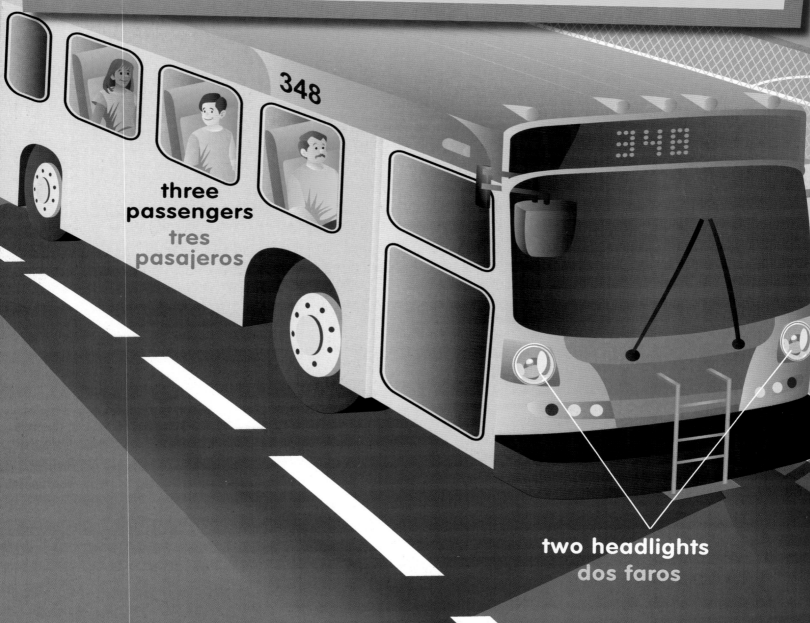

348

three passengers
tres pasajeros

two headlights
dos faros

42

five soccer players
cinco jugadores de fútbol

one dog
un perro

FRUIT STAND

68 54
348

four grocery bags
cuatro bolsas de compras

six oranges
seis naranjas

43

Games   Juegos

The grid on page 45 shows many different shapes and objects. Look carefully at the grid and follow the instructions below.

La cuadrícula de la página 45 muestra muchas formas y objetos diferentes. Mira con atención la cuadrícula y sigue las instrucciones que aparecen a continuación.

1. Count the birds.
2. Count the trucks.
3. Count the baseballs.
4. Count the blue markers.
5. Count the green markers.
6. Count the flowers.
7. Count the animals with four legs.
8. Count all of the animals.
9. Count the things you can eat.
10. Count all of the musical instruments.
11. Count all of the red objects.
12. Count all of the blue objects.
13. Count the things you can find in nature.
14. Count the things that are made by people.
15. Name the object that is shown only once.

1. Cuenta los pájaros.
2. Cuenta los camiones.
3. Cuenta las pelotas de béisbol.
4. Cuenta los marcadores azules.
5. Cuenta los marcadores pannds.
6. Cuenta las flores.
7. Cuenta los animales con cuatro patas.
8. Cuenta todos los animales.
9. Cuenta las cosas que se pueden comer.
10. Cuenta todos los instrumentos musicales.
11. Cuenta todos los objetos rojos.
12. Cuenta todos los objetos azules.
13. Cuenta las cosas que encontramos en la naturaleza.
14. Cuenta las cosas hechas por las personas.
15. Nombra el objeto que se muestra sólo una vez.

Look again!
¡Mira de nuevo!

These two pictures are not exactly the same. Can you find the eight things that are different in the second picture?

Estos dos dibujos no son exactamente iguales. ¿Puedes encontrar las ocho diferencias en el segundo dibujo?

Word-building activities
Actividades para el desarrollo del vocabulario

As your child's first teacher, you play an important role in nurturing your young learner's vocabulary development, one of the five essential steps that children must master in order to read. Here are some tips for promoting vocabulary development and reading success at home.

1. Make reading *My Book of Numbers* a warm, pleasant experience. Sit close to your child, snuggle, laugh, and have fun as you read aloud.

2. Practice counting with your child at every opportunity. How many trees in your yard? How many toys on your bed? How many shoes in your closet?

3. Practice one-on-one correspondence—an important math concept—with your child by asking him or her to make sure there is one spoon for each bowl, or one plate for each person.

4. Practice sorting into categories—another important math concept—by asking your child to match similar objects in everyday tasks. For example, you might have your child help you empty the dishwasher and sort the silverware.

5. Notice and talk about numbers that appear in your neighborhood or when traveling. For example, you could point out numbers on mailboxes or on license plates.

6. Point out everyday activities that use "math talk", such as when measuring ingredients, comparing sizes, adding milk to cereal, or taking away an extra spoon. "Math talk" language includes words such as *more, less, longer, biggest, adding, taking away, altogether, first, next, last,* etc.

Activities like these build the necessary groundwork for your child to connect information with printed words. Now your child is ready to take the next step to becoming a reader!

Usted es el primer maestro de su niño así que usted tiene un papel muy importante en estimular el desarrollo del vocabulario, este es uno de los pasos esenciales para que los niños puedan aprender a leer. Aquí tiene algunos consejos para promover el desarrollo del vocabulario y el éxito de la lectura en el hogar.

1. Cree un ambiente agradable y acogedor cuando lea el libro *My Book of Numbers*. Siéntese cerca de su niño, acurrúquese, ríanse y diviértanse juntos mientras usted lee en voz alta.

2. Cuente objetos de la casas para practicar el contar, como cuantos zapatos hay en el closet.

3. Practique las relaciones de uno a uno. Pídale a su niño que se asegure de poner una cuchara en cada plato o de darle un plato a cada persona. Este es un concepto importante de la matemática.

4. Practique el separar objetos en categorías. Este es otro concepto importante de la matemática. Por ejemplo, su niño puede agrupar los cubiertos de comer y juguetes de acuerdo a su tipo y tamaño.

5. Cuando estén en el vecindario enséñele los números en los buzones, letreros y licencias de los carros.

6. Practique el usar palabras de la matemática cuando este midiendo y comparando tamaños de diferentes objetos. Use palabras como *mas, menos, largo, más grande, añadir, quitar, juntos, primero, al lado, ultimo,* etc.